The
Great Ice Age

Library Edition Published 1990

Published by Marshall Cavendish Corporation
147 West Merrick Road
Freeport, Long Island
N.Y. 11520

Printed in Hong Kong by Colorcraft Ltd.

Designed and produced by
AS Publishing

Library of Congress Cataloging-in-Publication Data

Head, John G. (John Gerald)
  The great Ice age / by John G. Head : illustrated by Bernard Robinson.
    p. cm. — (Ages of the Earth)
  "First published 1989 by Cherrytree Press Ltd."- T.p. verso.
  Summary: A brother and sister travel back in time to several epochs in the Cenozoic Era and observe a variety of prehistoric mammals in their natural envioronment.
  ISBN 1-85435-188-5 ISBN 1-85435-182-6 (set)
  1. Glacial epoch — Juvenile literature. 2. Mammals, Fossil — Juvenile literature. [1. Glacial epoch. 2. Mammals, Fossil.] I. Robinson, Bernard, 1930- ill. II. Title. III. Series: Head, John G. (John Gerald). Ages of the earth.
  QE697.H39 1989
  569-dc20   89-34142
                                                      CIP
                                                      AC

AGES OF THE EARTH

The Great Ice Age

John G. Head
Illustrated by Bernard Robinson

MARSHALL CAVENDISH
NEW YORK · LONDON · TORONTO · SYDNEY

Mike and his sister Helen were traveling on the first Space-Time Shuttle. Two weeks before, they had set off to explore the prehistoric world. The highlight of their trip had been seeing the dinosaurs in the Mesozoic world. Now, they were about to embark on the last of their adventures.

As the Shuttle emerged from the blackness of time mode, the earth came into view.

"Gosh!" said Mike. "The world's changed completely. The land has split up."

Where there had once been a single land mass surrounded by an ocean, there were now separate continents.

"Where are we going to land?" asked Helen.

5

"America!" demanded Mike.

"Okay!" said Bob, the Shuttle's captain.

Mike usually got his own way. He had won the trip as a prize in a contest for children all over the world. His big sister was his guest on the "ticket-for-two."

Thanks to the knowledge of the Space-Time Ranger, Jenny Andrews, and the Shuttle's holographic computer, Timcom, the children were now experts on dinosaurs. After their visit to the Cretaceous Period, they were convinced that they knew why the dinosaurs had died out: the world's climate had grown too cold for the cold-blooded dinosaurs to survive.

"Mammals, like you," said Timcom, "have warm blood. Your body temperature stays much the same whatever the weather. Reptiles are only as warm as their surroundings."

"Mammals also have hair to keep them warm," said Jenny, "and they give birth to live young and feed them on milk. So young mammals are not in as much danger as reptiles, which hatch from eggs."

"Birds lay eggs," said Mike. "Why didn't they die out?"

"Feathers!" sighed Helen. "And they are warm-blooded." She could not understand why everyone thought her brother was so clever.

By now, they were coming in to land. Lieutenant "Atty" Atkins was at the controls. He was the Shuttle's second-in-command. Below them was thick forest stretching for miles. They zoomed over the treetops until the trees gave way to clear land.

"What time is it?" asked Helen.

"About 11," said Mike.

"Silly boy," said Helen. "What prehistoric time is it?"

"Early Eocene Epoch in the Cenozoic Era, some 50 million years before your time," said Timcom as they touched down.

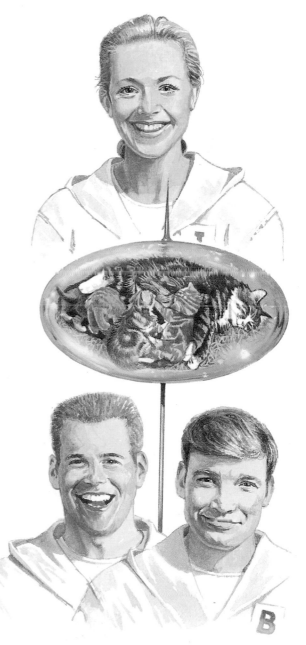

7

Everyone was expecting to be bored in the Cenozoic. Nothing could live up to the dinosaurs for excitement. Mike and Helen put on their protective suits, ready to explore. Atty and Jenny went with them. They all carried stun guns in case they met the unexpected.

The four walked for a mile and saw nothing. It was Timcom who pointed them in the right direction over the intercom.

"Look behind you!" said the computer. "That Diatryma has been trotting along behind you for half a mile." Before the robotic words were uttered, Mike and Helen and Atty had taken to their heels.

8

Diatryma

The three were hotly pursued by a huge, fat bird.

"Calm down," yelled Jenny, motioning to the others to stop. "It's only curious. It won't hurt us."

Sure enough, when they stopped the bird stopped. It had never seen anything like them nor they anything like it.

Suddenly, they heard something move. The bird put its head to one side. It had lost interest in the visitors from the twenty-first century. It could hear its lunch rustling. Its powerful legs went into action, speeding across the plain, just one stride behind whatever little creature ran ahead in a vain attempt to escape from the huge beak.

Jenny, who was doing important research, wanted to see the earliest ancestor of the horse, which lived during the Eocene. Later that day, they moved the Shuttle and landed as near as they safely could to a forest.

The forest was wonderful. As they explored, they caught glimpses of colorful birds and monkeys in the branches, and little scampering mammals in the undergrowth. Every time anyone made the slightest noise, Jenny scolded them.
   "Be careful where you walk. Just keep your eyes peeled."
The forest was growing darker and darker. It was hard to see at all, but there was not much chance of anyone missing a horse!

Over the intercom, Bob ordered everyone back to the Shuttle. Jenny told the others to go on. She ignored Bob's command and walked further into the forest. Before long, it was completely dark, and she had no idea how to get back to the Shuttle. Timcom gave her directions, and she stumbled after the others. She knew Bob would be furious.

Following Timcom's instructions, she picked her way through the undergrowth. Suddenly, the computer warned her to freeze. A shaft of moonlight pierced the trees. In the silvery light stood a little mammal.

   "It's a dog!" said Mike, who was watching the scene on Timcom's screen inside the Shuttle.
   "No, it's not," said Timcom. "It's a small ancestor of the horse. It's called an Eohippus."

Eohippus

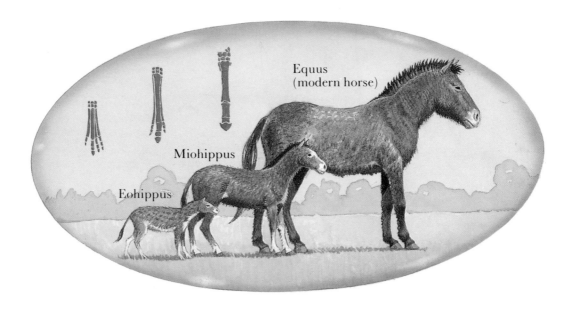

Jenny was soon forgiven for disobeying orders. She was overjoyed to have seen the little horse. She stayed rooted to the spot while Timcom photographed the shy creature taking its evening meal of leaves. Only after it had disappeared, and the moon had hidden itself once more, was she persuaded to return to the Shuttle.

Timcom explained to the others that the Eohippus had lived in the forest, but its descendants lived in open country. Miohippus, Merychippus and Pliohippus were all ancestors of Equus, the horse. Each one was bigger than the last. Their legs were longer and stronger; they needed speed to escape from enemies. Their teeth changed, too, so that they could eat grass instead of leaves. He showed them a picture of Miohippus compared with Eohippus and a modern horse.

Indricotherium

Now everyone wanted to see a
Miohippus. They had their
opportunity when they moved
on to the Oligocene Epoch the
following day. It was much
bigger than an Eohippus, but
not nearly as large as a creature
they saw when Atty took the
Shuttle on a trip to Asia.

It was an Indricotherium, the
largest land mammal that ever
lived. It was as tall as a giraffe,
but much heavier. It was
grazing on the treetops.

Moropus

Mike was astonished. These animals were proving almost as exciting as dinosaurs. Indricotherium was a giant rhinoceros. Mike wanted to stay where they were and see some more, but Jenny wanted to go back to North America and move on to Miocene times to find a Merychippus. Sadly, they failed to find one for her, but, happily, they saw another giant called Moropus.

While they were having lunch, as usual squeezed from a tube, Jenny told them how the horse migrated from North America to Europe and Asia during the Pliocene Epoch.

"Perhaps your Merychippus has already gone," said Bob. "Let's go and see if we can find some horses in Asia."

It took less than an hour to travel the few million years to the Pliocene Epoch. They landed in lush green countryside.

Bored with looking for horses, Helen persuaded Mike to lag behind the others.

"Let's take our helmets off," she said. "It would be so nice to breathe some fresh air. There are all these wonderful plants, and we'll have to go back to our own time, never having smelled them."

Mike, who had taken his whole suit off once and come to no harm, readily agreed. Timcom would know immediately and raise an alarm, but they didn't care.

The sun was warm, and they really could smell the scent of flowers in the air. They could also hear with their own ears a snuffling noise. It was coming from a creature that was scooping up whole plants from the soil.

"He looks dangerous," said Helen, jamming her helmet back on her head.

Platybelodon

"Whatever is it?" asked Mike, relieved to see Atty hurrying toward them in response to Timcom's alarm.

"It is a Platybelodon," said Timcom, its circuit restored. "If you had not been foolish enough to disconnect the intercom, I would have warned you of its presence. Now return to the Shuttle before it scoops you up, too." Atty, stun gun at the ready, stood guard over the Platybelodon – which was really quite harmless.

That afternoon, Mike and Helen had to stay in the Shuttle.

"You can watch the others exploring, but you cannot go out yourselves; you can't be trusted," said Bob.

"I'll stay with them," said Atty. "You and Jenny go and have a good time. I'm tired of rounding up horses."

Gigantopithecus

Mike was sulking and wouldn't talk to anyone. Helen had her head in a book, so Atty decided to have a snooze. He was awakened by a frantic Helen.

"Come and look at this," she said. "The others will never get back in. The Shuttle is surrounded by giant gorillas."

Mike and Atty hurried to look. Sure enough, a whole troop of apes was gathered around the hatch. Timcom was filming them and taking no notice of Helen's panic.

"They will soon get bored," said Timcom. "They are apes called Gigantopithecus."

"Are we descended from them?" asked Mike.

"Certainly not," said Timcom. "Human ancestors evolved in Africa, and they were much smaller even than you."

Timcom was right as usual. The huge apes did wander away, long before Jenny and Bob arrived back. They were both upset to have missed seeing a Gigantopithecus. There was so much to see, and they had so little time. Everyone knew they were getting to the end of their trip, so they made friends again and spent the evening playing word games with Timcom. During the night, they went into time mode and had landed in the Pleistocene long before the sleepers awoke.

"We know when we are, Timcom," said Helen, "but not where."

"You are in a South American rainforest," said the computer.

"This time, we'll all go out," said Bob. "Timcom is perfectly capable of guarding the Shuttle. He can even make it take off without us!"

The forest was alive with butterflies, spiders and wonderful beetles. The plants were thick and green.

"There's still some forest like this left in our own time," said Jenny. "What a pity that people destroy it."

"I'll bet it hasn't got creatures like that in it," said Atty. He was staring at a huge, shaggy sloth.

"Or like that!" said Mike. "It's like a great big tank."

"That is not a tank," said Timcom through the intercom. "It is a giant armadillo. There are creatures like it today, but they are considerably smaller. Unlike the horse, Glyptodon's descendants got gradually smaller. The same is true of the giant sloth Megatherium. There are several species of sloth in your own time – though they are not quite so big."

Megatherium

Glyptodon

Robinson

They spent the whole day in the rainforest and voted it their best day. Mike and Helen agreed that the giant sloth was the one animal they would take home if they could.

They almost couldn't find the Shuttle when they returned.
    "Perhaps Timcom has gone without us," said Mike.
    "The craft is straight in front of you," said the computer. "A few creepers have grown over it during the day, that is all. Plants grow fast in this part of the world because it is so hot and wet."

Instead of spending the night in the forest, Bob and Atty decided to take the Shuttle farther north. From space, they saw a great change in the lands below. Instead of forests, there were small clumps of trees. They flew over the North Pole and saw how huge the polar ice cap had become since their arrival in the Cenozoic Period.

20

Timcom showed them a map. There was ice over most of Europe and over the top half of North America. They stayed in earth orbit until morning. When they landed, it was snowing, and the ground was icy.

"That's what the snowshoes were for!" said Helen.

"Don't take your helmet off today," said Bob, "or your ears will freeze off. And don't go far from the Shuttle. There are dangerous animals out there."

He was right; they didn't get far. In fact, they all fled back to the craft immediately, followed by two vicious-looking big cats.

"Those are scimitar cats," said Timcom. "I expect they are hungry."

Scimitar cats

Back inside the Shuttle, Timcom told them about the Great Ice Age, when it was so cold that great glaciers crept across the landscape, with animals moving south to escape the cold. Several times, the climate grew warmer, and for thousands of years, the ice retreated again, followed by the animals.

"Can we go and see what it was like then?" asked Mike.

"Why not!" said Bob. "Timcom can pinpoint a good time."

The Shuttle went into time mode, and soon they were in what is now sunny California. It was sunny then, too, so they went out to explore.

"Look at that lake over there," said Mike running toward a shimmering pool. "There's an elephant swimming in it."

Saber-toothed cat

Mike ran headlong toward the water. Timcom told him to stop, but he ignored the warning. A huge, elephant-like creature called a Mastodon was wallowing in the water. But it wasn't water! Mike found out too late. It was a pool of tar. A layer of water on the top made it look like a lake. The edges of the pool were soft and slippery. Mike ended up like the Mastodon, wallowing in the sticky tar.

Atty and Jenny ran back to the Shuttle to get a rope. They met Bob, who had heard the alarm. In moments, they were back at the pool. There, they found a newcomer, a fierce saber-toothed cat. It was running toward Helen, who was trying to reach her brother.

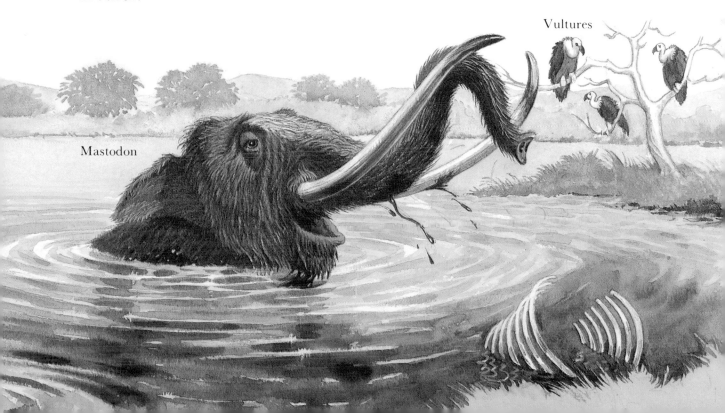

Vultures

Mastodon

The rescuers didn't know what to do first. Jenny aimed her stun gun at the cat and stopped it in its tracks. Atty grabbed Helen and stopped her from falling into the pool. Bob threw Mike a rope and managed to haul him out.

So much for California! Mike was covered in tar. It took hours to clean it off. All the time, they could hear the trumpeting of the poor Mastodon. Nothing could save him. Like Mike, he had thought it was a waterhole and had become trapped. Had the great cat had its chance, it would have plunged into the pool to attack the Mastodon. Then it, too, would have been trapped.

"There are many fossilized animals from those pools. Mike was one of thousands to make the mistake!" said Jenny.

"Tar is a very good preservative," said Timcom.

"It doesn't feel that way when you are up to your neck in it," said Mike.

Diprotodon
(wombat)

"Can we go somewhere nice now," asked Helen, "where we won't be attacked?"

"Okay!" said Bob. "Let's try sunny Australia."

They zoomed south and landed on a great red plain. There were lots and lots of animals. They hovered for a while, following great herds of kangaroos, gentle giants leaping along in their hundreds. They all felt safe enough to leave the Shuttle. They were rewarded by the sight of a Procoptodon. The great kangaroo was nursing her little joey (not so little; it was the size of Mike). Nearby, there was a huge wombat. Immediately, Helen deserted the giant sloth. She would have to have a prehistoric wombat!

Procoptodon
(kangaroo)

"Australian mammals are quite different from other mammals," Timcom told them that evening. "They are mainly marsupials. When they give birth, their babies are tiny. They have to be kept safe in a pouch attached to their mother's body."

Before floating off to sleep that night, Helen dreamed of owning a wombat.

The next day was the last one of their trip. They landed in Europe, on the edge of a glacier. The whole world was white. Mike pleaded to be allowed out. But Bob was worried. They were all still alive. He didn't want any nasty accidents on their last day.

As usual, Mike won the battle of wills. They took stun guns and trudged over the snowy wastes in their snowshoes. Suddenly, they saw a magnificent sight. It was a great, hairy mammoth.
    "Ice is a great preserver," said Timcom. "Many fossilized mammoths have been found in Siberia under the Arctic ice."

Nobody was listening. They were too entranced by the sight of the great beast plodding heavily toward them. It had its calf by its side. Helen forgot the wombat. She had to have the baby mammoth.

Suddenly, disaster struck. The baby mammoth appeared to slip on the ice. Timcom sounded a warning, and Bob hurried everyone back to the Shuttle. But they did not get that far.

Wooly mammoth

They could not see what Timcom could see. The baby mammoth had not slipped. It had been struck by a spear with a flint head. A new creature had appeared. It was small, hairy and stealthy. It was a human being.

"Keep down," said Bob. "Do not let those men see us. They are dangerous. They are fiercer hunters than the great cats."

"But what about the great mammoth and its calf," said Mike. "We must save them."

"Nothing can save them," said Jenny. "People have to live, too, and they need meat to eat in this cold wilderness. We must go now, back to our own time, and leave these humans to their history."

AGES OF THE EARTH TOUR

Shuttle back in time and see with your own eyes 600 million years of Earth's history in just three weeks.

Periods	Years Ago (Millions)	Plants and Animals
Pre-cambrian	4,500	No life on Earth to start with. Tiny plants appear about 3,000 million years ago in the sea; first known animals appear about 700 million years ago.
Cambrian	600	No life on land, but in the sea there are creatures called graptolites and trilobites, corals and sponges, shellfish and jellyfish.
Ordovician	500	More graptolites and trilobites in sea. Creatures called brachiopods, and the first fish – which have armor.
Silurian	440	Land plants appear. Lots of fish in the sea and giant sea-scorpions.
Devonian	395	The age of fishes. Sea teems with all kinds, including huge jawed fish and sharks. Small creatures leave the sea to live on land. Amphibians evolve from fish.
Carboniferous	345	Giant land plants in coal swamps. Large amphibians and the first insects, including some giants. Reptiles evolve from amphibians.
Permian	280	Lots more reptiles and fewer amphibians. Trilobites die out.

PALEOZOIC ERA

AGES OF THE EARTH TOUR

Visit each of these periods and see the animals and plants of bygone ages, monsters of land and sea and sky.

	Periods	Years Ago (Millions)	Plants and Animals
MESOZOIC ERA	Triassic	225	The first dinosaurs. Large reptiles and shelled creatures called ammonites in the sea. Mammals evolve from reptiles.
	Jurassic	200	Lots of dinosaurs, including huge sauropods and carnosaurs. Pterosaurs in the air. Birds evolve from reptiles.
	Cretaceous	135	New kinds of dinosaurs, including ones with armor. Small mammals and birds. First flowering plants. At the end of the period, dinosaurs and many other creatures die out.
CENOZOIC ERA	Tertiary	65	The age of mammals. Many kinds of mammals evolve, including horses, elephants, and apes. Coniferous forests and grasslands.
	Quaternary	2	Mammoths, wooly mammoths and saber-toothed cats live through Ice Ages. Ancestors of humans appear. The first humans appear.

Index